WordPress For Beginners

The Simple Guide to Learning WordPress For Website Development Fast!

Copyright 2015

Table Of Contents

Introduction

I want to thank you and congratulate you for downloading the book 'WordPress For Beginners'. This book will help you to build an impressive website using all of the features WordPress has to offer, and hopefully inspire you to continue learning about WordPress and all of the wonderful features available.

This book contains proven steps and strategies on how to become a true master of building simple websites on WordPress that will wow your customers. Not only does this book teach you how to build a website using WordPress, but it also walks you through the process of registering a domain name and setting up web-hosting services. Everything you need to build your website and get it online is included in this book.

In this technologically driven modern world, you will need a professional website to connect your business to your customers. Gone are the days of flipping through the Yellow Pages. Today people go to their computers when they need products or services, and WordPress provides an easy and affordable way to put your business in front of those customers. You need customers to be able to find you online, and customers will appreciate the convenience of having a well executed website that they can visit for information and other services.

If you do not develop your business to work within the technology of today's world, you will be left behind. New customers won't be able to find you, and you will miss out on the opportunity to grow your business. The Internet is a fantastic resource that should not be treated lightly. Nothing else today can help you grow your business as quickly as the Internet. Don't take a chance on losing a customer because they couldn't find you online. The bottom line is that for many customers, if you don't exist online, you don't exist at all. There is nothing worse for a business than not existing to their customer base. Don't let that happen to you. Get your website up now, before the next customer can't find you.

It's time for you to become an amazing business that also has an amazing website! Use the simple steps in this book to build your website using WordPress today. There is absolutely nothing you can do that will raise your company's profile faster than create a well organized and visually pleasing website. Online marketing is one of the fastest growing industries for a reason, and that reason is that online is where the customers are. You can't get the customers to come to you if you don't go to them first. Put yourself online. Your customers are waiting for you.

Chapter One:
Wordpress.com vs. Wordpress.org

Many people think that they can get a free site on wordpress.com and get all of the functions of wordpress.org. However, wordpress.com is a site dedicated to supporting blogs. Now, if you are looking to improve your web exposure and boost your search results, a blog is a good way to do that and wordpress.com is a fantastic resource for accomplishing this goal.

However, if you want to design a website using all of the features that has made WordPress famous, you will need a wordpress.org site. The .org sites are designed to do business, and contain the plugins that will make it easy to set your website up to function as another way of doing business. Using this option, your webpage will look professional and will have all of the functionality you need from your site.

You absolutely cannot do business on a wordpress.com site. You can set up contact forms for clients to contact you, but you are absolutely forbidden from selling anything on it. The only way to earn revenue from a wordpress.com site is to gain a large blog following and earn money off of the advertising. However, earning ad revenue from a blog is likely not your industry, and not a practical way of growing your business.

However, there are some things that you need to keep in mind when hosting your own site. For instance, you will be responsible for completing backups and keeping up on the site maintenance yourself. There are several plugins that can help you with the backups and you can even set up an automatic backup to take place at regular intervals, but it will be one more responsibility for someone in your business. A lack of commitment to completing maintenance and backups on your website leave you vulnerable to site crashes that will be difficult to repair.

Maintenance includes tasks like updating your site, checking for dead links (yep, there's a plugin for that), deleting the spam comments (there is a plugin for that too!), validating your site on a regular basis, checking your stats, checking your linkability, submitting site changes to search engines if you have done a major overhaul on your site, and updating your advertising.

For maintenance, keep a regular schedule to stay on track. For instance, you could use something like this:

Update WordPress:

WordPress is constantly adding new features and functionality. To keep your website up to date, you should update your WordPress site two to four times a year.

Checking For Dead Links:

Sometimes links change or maybe you misspelled a permalink. Users of your site will not appreciate being directed to a virtual dead end, and will become quickly disengaged. You have one chance to hook a customer with your website. If you fail on the first attempt, you likely won't have an opportunity to get a second attempt. You can check to see if any of these 404-Page Not Found messages are contaminating your site by using a dead links tool.

Do A WordPress Check In:

Check the WordPress website to find any upgrades or other events you need to know about.

Delete Spam Comments:

If you have a blog on your site, you can use Askimet plugin to filter out the spam comments. When you install your site, this plugin will already be installed and active. Filtering the spam is recommended, as no one reading your blog wants to wade through a pool of spam to find out what insights other readers have on the topic. A clean comment section will engage readers to interact with your website, and each other. This will help to create a community on your site, and the extra activity will help you in your search rankings. Google loves sites with a lot of chatter going on.

Back Up Your Site:

You should have a plugin that is taking care of the backups on your server, but you should also do backups on your computer too. Depending on how much new content you add on a monthly basis, you will probably want to do this somewhere between three to twelve times a year.

Updating Your Site:

Updating your site includes adding new content. Websites with fresh content get higher search results, which is why having a blog on your site is a good idea. It is a good way to tell customers about upcoming products or changes you are making to your services, passing along information about changes to your industry, and it gives you an easy way to add content that will keep your site fresh and relevant. The activity generated by adding new content on a regular basis shows the search engines that you are an active and relevant site.

Validating Your Site, Again:

If you have made any major changes to your site, you need to take the time to go through the validation process again to make sure it is still running smoothly. You can also schedule validation tests to take place on a set schedule. If you have made no major changes to the site, you should complete the validation process once a year. You can use any browser's link checker or a variety of free online websites that you can find in a simple Google search.

Check Your Stats:

Hovering breathlessly over your stats page is a waste of time, but you do want to check your stats on a regular basis to ensure you are reaching your target audience. Your stats will tell you what is working, and what isn't. The stats show you what pages are most viewed, who are viewing them, and where they are being directed to your site from. This is useful information in knowing how to drive traffic to your site. After all, all the work to set up a site is for people to see it. This information will tell you the people that are most interested in your site and where you can find them.

Determine Your Likability:

Search engines like pages that other pages have linked back to. If others link to your site, it means that they found it helpful and sites like Google love that. You can Google "link popularity" to find sites that will tell you if anyone has been linking back to your site and who they are. This should be done somewhere between three to twelve times a year.

Submit Your Site To Search Engines:

That's right. You don't have to wait for the search engines to notice you. You can submit your shiny new website directly to the search engines using a variety of tools. Just search "submit site" and you will find a plethora of tools to help you gain visibility with search engines and customers/users. However, this comes with a word of caution, as you shouldn't do this more than once a year. Repeated submissions to the same search engine can actually harm you, as you will be dinged by the search engine and lowered in search rankings. Once a year is sufficient, and the search engines will welcome your submission annually.

Now, all of this information may have your head swimming. It is easy to feel overwhelmed when you first see everything that goes into maintaining a website. However, many of these tasks can be automated and the rest will only take a few minutes of your time. Don't let the to-do list of keeping a website performing well intimidate you; you can do this.

Chapter Two:
What Do You Want Your Website To Do?

Before you begin building your website, you need to decide exactly what you want it to do. Are you using it as a way to reach new customers and provide information? Will you sell products on your site? Do you want customers to be able to schedule appointments from your website? Do you want the ability to generate an email list? Do you want to include a photo gallery of products or maybe some pictures of your team working hard? It is a lot to think about, but having an idea of what you need from your website before you begin will help you when it comes to designing the look, layout and functionality of your new website.

A well planned website will make the process of building the site a lot easier, and it will save you countless hours of going back to redo something. If you do not have a good idea of how you want the website to look and function, you will likely spend a lot of time changing things that you have already completed, causing you to redo the same thing several times. It is not an efficient approach, and it will be easy to get frustrated and feel like you aren't ever going to finish the site.

WordPress has many options for how a website functions. Knowing what you need from your WordPress site will help you to choose the plugins you need, and avoid the ones that you don't. Too many plugins can be difficult to manage, and can sometimes create more problems than they solve. You should definitely use plugins, but you might want to be a bit judicious in deciding which ones to use. Try to only use plugins that add value to your site. Too many functions on a website can make it confusing and difficult to use.

A good way to stay on track when setting up your website is to use a checklist. This will help you get things done in the order that makes the most sense, and help you to avoid missing any steps.

Below is a checklist for setting up a WordPress website. Each step has had an entire chapter devoted to it, and we will go into more detail there. However, to give you an idea of what each step is please see the list below.

Domain Name:

This is the step where you will choose and purchase your domain name. You will learn how to choose between a .com, .net and .org, how keywords and your domain name are connected, where you can register your domain name, and how much it costs.

Web Hosting:

During this stage, you will set up hosting services on a server. We will give you the tools you need to evaluate different hosting company's reputations and the plans they offer, provide you with the questions you should ask when choosing a web-hosting company, and how much this will cost.

Install WordPress:

This is the step where you install WordPress onto your server. Included are automatic installer instructions and instructions for installing manually using a variety of software.

Install Theme:

This is the fun part because this is where you get to begin building your site's appearance. You will learn where you can find themes, how to download them, and how to customize them.

Set Up Content:

Content includes text, pictures, video and logos. This is anything you add to your site. We will help you add content and set up a static homepage. In this section, we also discuss the function of pages, and the value they add to your site.

In addition to these steps, you will also find a chapter at the end that is devoted entirely to plugins. Plugins add functionality to your site and take care of some routine maintenance issues. With over 37,000 different plugins, you are sure to find the exact thing your site needs to impress customers.

Take some time to do some research. Visit websites of other companies in your industry and take a look at how their websites are set up. Take note of the functionality that is included. You don't want to copy a website completely, but taking a few good ideas and incorporating them into your site is a good way to get started. As you move forward, you may decide that certain functions aren't as useful as you thought they would be, and you will remove them or change them out for another function that you think will work better. Building a website is a little bit of trial and error. Do your best to enjoy the journey and learn what works. Soon you will have a fabulous website that will wow even the most reluctant customer.

Chapter Three:
Choose and Register A Domain Name

Choosing a domain name is much like choosing the name of your business. It needs to be catchy, easy to remember and something that represents your business well.

To make this easier, these tips can help you choose the perfect domain name:

Keep It Short:

Long names are confusing and difficult to remember. Customers are more likely to misspell a long name or not be able to remember it at all, which can make you difficult to find in the vast abyss of the Internet. Keep it short and sweet, and your customers will remember your domain name.

No Plurals Or Hyphens, And Avoid Abbreviations:

These kinds of tactics can confuse customers. Unless your business name uses a plural or abbreviation, don't use them. And never, ever, use a hyphen. Even Wal-Mart doesn't use the hyphen in their domain name. If Wal-Mart doesn't need it, you don't either. This has to be easy to remember, so keep it simple.

Domain Names Are Branding:

The domain name you choose will have a huge impact on your branding. Regardless of you being an established business or a start-up, the branding on your website must match the branding of your business, which has to match the branding of your social media, business cards, brochures, and everything else that has your business name on it. Never underestimate the power of branding, and the substantial effect your domain name will have in your marketing strategies.

Get a .com If You Can:

The Internet was built with .coms, and people have not forgotten. People will type in a domain address and end it with .com without giving it a second thought, until an unfamiliar website appears on their screen. If it is a first time visitor to your site, they will likely give up on you and move on to a site that is easier to find. Habits are hard to break, and many of the highest traffic websites end in a .com. Some people think that this is because the .coms get better search results because search engines favor URLs that end in .com, but that is absolutely not true. Search engines treat domain names the same regardless of whether they end in .com, .org or .net. The reason a .com site receives more traffic has to do with how well they have positioned themselves online. If the .com has anything to do with it, it is because it is the familiar way to end a URL, not because a search engine favors a .com.

Do Your Due Diligence And Verify That Your Domain Name Is Not A Trademark Registered To Someone else:

Trademarks are a serious business, and you don't want to accidently use someone else's trademarked material. Using someone else's trademarked material, even if it is an accident, can be a costly mistake. This mistake can quickly become a legal nightmare, costing you thousands of dollars in attorney's fees, legal fees, and fines. An easy way to avoid this is to go to www.uspto.gov and check your domain name. If it is registered as someone else's intellectual property, this site will tell you. Protect yourself, and your business, by taking a couple of minutes to make sure you are within your legal rights to use the domain name you have chosen.

Register Domain Names Immediately:

Once you fall in love with the perfect domain name, don't take a lackadaisical approach to registering it. Get over to a domain registration site and lock that name down before someone else claims ownership of your brilliant name. Registering a domain name is fast and easy. It is also fast and easy for someone else to register it if you don't get there first.

Don't Use Prefixes:

Prefixes include http:// and www. Search engines no longer require these prefixes, and including them can lead to potential customers receiving a "site not found" message. Leaving them off doesn't prevent people from finding you if they include the prefixes in the URL.

Your Domain Name Is Also A Keyword:

When choosing your domain name, you also need to consider the keywords you include. The keywords you choose to include will influence your search results, and should carefully consider this when choosing a name. SEO will have a substantial impact on new customers finding you via search results, and you want to make sure you are one of the first results they see. Don't forget that your domain name is a major keyword.

The registration process for a domain name is incredibly easy, and there are many places you can purchase domain names from. Check around and see if anyone is offering any deals. Web-hosting companies will often give you a deal when you sign up, and you should check with them before you decide where to register your domain name. You can also find discounts located on websites and YouTube videos that post tutorials about setting up websites. Many of the people that do these tutorials have a large following, and are given their own coupon codes by the hosting companies that can be used by anyone. Many of these coupon codes offer savings of up to 30%; others will get you the first month of service for a penny. With the price of domain registration and web-hosting services already being so affordable, coupon codes that offer these kinds of savings can make your startup cost you almost nothing.

Once you have registered your domain name, you will need to periodically renew it to maintain ownership. How often you need to renew it will depend on the package you choose. Most domain registration sites, even if located on hosting services, will offer the option to auto renew, and will automatically withdraw the fee from the payment account you provided when you set up the domain name. Auto renew is the recommended method to protect your domain name from expiring. Once your domain name expires, someone else could take ownership from you and there is nothing you can do. Auto renew is the best protection you have against this scenario.

You will also need to keep your email address up to date. Domain renewal notices are emailed to you, and give you the opportunity to take care of any payment issues quickly. You risk losing your domain name if you miss out on a chance to take care of a problem quickly, as the domain name is up for grabs if your account becomes suspended. Once someone else has that domain name, there is no recovering it.

Chapter Four:
Set Up Your Web Hosting

Setting up web hosting can seem intimidating. Many people believe that this is complicated and requires a lot of technical knowhow. That used to be true, but the technology is now so advanced that you need very little technical know how to set up and manage a server.

Web-hosting companies offer a variety of discounts and pricing packages. Be sure to read through the options and decide what package right for you. You can sign up for an account online, and choose the package that will provide you with all of the services and support that you need. Some packages will come with free or substantially discounted domain name registration, free email accounts and more.

There are many hosting companies to choose from, and there are a few things you should consider before you decide on one. To make this process easier, we have included a list of some things to consider before you commit to any hosting company.

When Choosing A Web Hosting Company Consider:

Your Needs:

Looking at a list of best web hosting providers has no practical application if you don't know what you need from a server. Different websites will need different things from a server. For instance, a blog will require much less umph from a server than an e-commerce site. If you have any questions on what kind of muscle you need from your server, you can contact the hosting company through email, live chat, or telephone (depending on the company). Most sites find that a small shared-hosting account with a hosting company that has a good reputation takes care of their needs. Shared hosting accounts are very simple to work with, easy to maintain and are the most affordable option.

Server Uptime:

Server Uptime is exactly what it sounds like; it is the amount of time that the server (and your website) is up. Ideally, the server will always be up. However, life isn't perfect and sometimes things go haywire. Your mission is to find the hosting company that has the best record for keeping websites live. The last thing you want is for a customer to get frustrated because they can't get to your site. You can find a hosting companies record for uptime on many review websites, and on uptime monitoring sites. Take the time to look through these and evaluate the companies carefully. Your website is worthless if your hosting company can't keep it live.

Multiple Domains:

You may not need multiple domains today, but what about tomorrow? As your website grows, you may want to add more domains like a sister site that will help boost your search rankings. This also allows you to register domain names that are similar to yours that will catch misdirected customers and allow you to save the sale. It might cost a dollar or two more to sign up for a package with multiple domains, but it is worth the investment.

Upgrade Options:

If you notice a substantial increase in the number of unique visitors you are getting to your site or you are adding on functions that will require more server space, it is time to look at a VPS or dedicated server. These servers will give you more advanced security features, and better processing power to prevent your site from being slow. You will also receive an increase in disk storage and memory capacity. Talk to your hosting company to discuss the functions on your website, and the kind of server you will need to support your site. Your hosting company will be able to steer you in the right direction.

Read The Terms Of Service:

You should do this for a couple of reasons. First of all, when you first sign up with the hosting company you will get rock bottom rates. However, after a year or two, you might notice your renewal rates begin to increase. This is an industry standard, and you are not being ripped off. These increases are generally only a few dollars at a time, and if you have a shared hosting account they tend to remain below $10.00 per month.

Reading the Terms of Service will also clue you into the restrictions the hosting company will place on you. Some are stricter than others, so it is worth taking the time to know what you are getting yourself into.

You also want to check the Terms of Service for transparency. You want to see clear guidelines that are explained well. Looking for these qualities in the Terms of Service will help you determine if the hosting company is trustworthy. After all, you are trusting them with your business and you want to make sure they are worthy of such an important responsibility.

What Is The Refund Policy?

Checking the refund policy is a good rule to follow when making any purchase, and purchasing web-hosting services is no exception. If you are dissatisfied with the service, it is important to know ahead of time how much it will cost you to get out of the contract. Avoid companies that have high cancellation fees. You can find hosting companies that will provide money back guarantees and will even allow you to request a pro-rated refund if you decide to cancel after the trial period.

Make Sure Basic Hosting Features Are Included:

Some companies are able to give a discounted price because they fail to provide basic features. Be sure your package includes these necessary features.

Cron: for all day-to-day operations

Auto Script Installer: These include Fantastico, Simple Scripts and Quick Installer. They are huge time savers!

.htacces: You will need this for page redirects and other security features.

SSI: This feature makes site maintenance easier.

FTP: You will need this for easy access to your files.

You can get away with not having these features if you choose WP Engine or another specialty host. Otherwise, if you don't see these basic features included in the package, keep shopping.

E-Commerce Support:

If you are selling products via an online store located on your site, you are going to need special features to support the e-commerce functions like online payment security and online shopping cart functions.

Look For:

SSL Certification

Dedicated IPs

Easy installations of shopping cart software.

Limits On Your Hosting Package:

You might risk having your account suspended if you start using too much CPU power. Read the rules carefully, and know what your limits are. If you see that your CPU usage is getting dangerously high, you will want to upgrade your services. Some hosting companies will notify you or offer flexible CPU usage packages.

Email Accounts:

Having an email account that is you@yourbusinessname.com looks professional and inspires customer confidence. Check to see if your package offers this service, and how many email accounts you can have. You usually have the option to purchase more if you need them for a reasonable price.

Subscription Period:

Some hosting companies require long commitments. However, you don't need to make a long-term commitment to get a good rate on server space. Shop around, and avoid long commitments.

Questions About Back Ups:

Websites crash, but if you have regular back ups set up you have nothing to worry about. The hosting company can easily restore a good copy of your site and have you up and running in no time. We have created a list of questions you need to ask to ensure you are prepared for such an event.

Are automated back ups available?

How easy are back ups to manage from the control panel?

Does the hosting company complete full back ups?

Are back up files easy to restore?

The answer to all of these questions should be "yes".

Easy To Use Control Panel:

You want a control panel that is easy to understand, and easy to use. Sure, the hosting company will help you, but it takes time to consult them every time you need to get something done on your site. Choose a hosting company with easy to use features, and a control panel that makes sense.

Since you will be using WordPress, you want to make sure that the cPanel offers easy options for downloading and installing your WordPress site directly onto the server. Paying attention to this detail will make your life a lot easier when it comes time to install WordPress. It probably goes without saying, but auto install is much easier than creating directories and installing the files manually.

If you don't have an auto install for WordPress, you will have to do it manually. While some people may have done some stuff like manual uploads in a computer class and feel comfortable with the process, others will be intimidated by the process and wish they had spent more time finding a web-hosting company with a cPanel that allowed for a one-click installation of WordPress. Check out Chapter Five: Installing

WordPress to see the manual instructions and decide if manual installment is something you think you can do. If you feel that you can't, auto install is going to be a requirement for you from the web-hosting company that you choose.

Client Support:

Look for a hosting company that has a variety of ways to contact them, and offers 24/7 support. Your website needs to be up and operating all the time, and you need access to people that can help you with that at any hour of any day.

To begin the process, you will need to create an account. You will need to create login information, a user name and include payment information. You will also be required to register or import a domain name if you purchased the domain from someone other than the hosting company. Then work through the steps that are outlined above to get set up on a hosting site that is perfect for you.

Choosing your web host is an important decision. It is the web host that will keep your website online. You are trusting them with your content, and with your customer's access to your website. That is a lot of trust. Thankfully there are several wonderful web-hosting companies out there, and a little research will help you choose the right company with confidence.

Chapter Five:
Install WordPress To Your Server

Once you have set up a web hosting account, you will need to install WordPress onto the server. Since you did the research outlined in the previous chapter, you have chosen a web host that has provided you with an easy to navigate cPanel.

You will need to login into your easy to use cPanel to install WordPress. This should be a very simple process that will take you less than five minutes. With most web-hosting companies, you will often be able to use a tool like Fantastico to automatically complete the install for you.

In some cases, you will have to do the install manually. While this can seem intimidating, all it really means is that you are going to download a zip file onto your computer and then upload those files onto the server. It will take a little longer than five minutes, but not much if you follow the instructions and pay attention to everything on the installation checklist that we are going to provide.

Before you begin installing, there is a checklist you need to go through first.

You will need:

- Access to your web server using shell or FTP

- A text editor

- A FTP client

- Your choice of web browser

You will also need to:

- Ensure that both you and your package on the web host have the necessary minimum requirements to successfully run WordPress.

- You will need to download the most current version of WordPress available.

- Once WordPress is downloaded onto your computer, you will need to unzip the zip file and create a folder on your hard drive to store the files in.

- Have a secure password prepared for your Secret Key

- Keep this page in a location that is easy to access during installation

Instructions For A Five-Minute Install:

Now, if you are not familiar with this type of installation, it will likely take you a little longer than five minutes. However, it won't take you much longer.

If you haven't downloaded the zip file and put the unzipped files into a folder on your hard drive, do that now.

- You will need to create a database on your server for WordPress, and a MySQL user with privileges to access and modify it.

- Find the wp-config-sample.php to wp-config.php file and rename it. Then edit the file to add your database information. (This step is optional and can be skipped.

The install program on the server will create the wp-confighp.php file without you completing this step.)

- Upload the files to the root of your domain. This will look like "http://yourwebsitename.com/". You will need to upload all of the contents of the unzipped files, excluding the WordPress directory file, onto the root directory of your server.

- Should you choose to upload the files onto its own subdirectory on your site, maybe you want to put it into a blog that would look something like http://yourwebsitename.com/blog/. First create the blog directory on your server, and then you can upload the unzipped files onto the directory by using FTP. If the FTP client you are using converts files into lower case, you should make sure it is disabled.

- Access the URL in a web browser, and run the WordPress installation script. This should be the same URL that you used to upload the files. If the files are located in the root directory, you will use http://www.yourwebsitename.com/. If you uploaded the files into a blog subdirectory, you will use http://yourwebsitename.com/blog/.

Ta da! You have just installed WordPress. You are a genius and the master of the webpage!

If that didn't do the trick, you may need some more detailed instructions. We are here to help, and have included more detailed instructions below. These instructions require some techy know how. If you have a little experience in these things, you will likely be able to follow the instructions with success. If any of this looks confusing, your hosting company will often help, but they will likely charge a fee.

This is where choosing a cPanel with that is easy to use becomes so important. If you have an auto install for WordPress, this is a very quick and painless process. In the examples below, manual installation can be very simple. However, depending on the processes you need to use, or if something doesn't go quite as planned, it can become an overwhelming and frustrating task.

Step 1: Download and Extract the WordPress Files

- If uploading WordPress to a remote server, you can download the WordPress zip file package directly onto your computer using a web browser. Once the download is complete, unzip the files and save them in a folder on your hard drive.

- If you will be using FTP, you can skip the next step.

- If you are using shell access to your server, you may wish to download WordPress directly to your server. You can use wget, lynx or any other console-based web browser to avoid using FTP.

  o Using Shell, this will look like wget http://wordpresss. Org/latest.tar.gz

  o You can then unzip the package using tar –xzve latest.tar.gz

  o The files will download into a folder titled WordPress in the same latest.tar.gz directory.

2. Create Database And User

- When using web hosting, you probably already have a WordPress database set up or you might have an automated setup option. You can check the hosting company's support page for an indication of what solutions your hosting company offers. You might also be able to find some indication on your cPanel.

- If you need to create a database manually, follow the instructions for Plesk, cPanel or phpMyAdmin located below.

- If you only have one database, you can still install WordPress on it, even if it is already being used. Just make sure you use a distinctive prefix to avoid over-writing and database tables that already exist.

Plesk:

- Log into Plesk.

- Go to the Custom Website area on the Website and Domains page and click **Database**.

- Click **Add New Database**. You have the option to change the database name here. You will need to create a database user, provide the credentials and then click **OK**.

cPanel:

- Log into the cPanel

- Under the Databases section, click on **MySQL Database Wizard**.

- Step 1: You will need to create a database by entering the name of the database and click **next step**.

- Step 2: You will need to create database users by entering the database user name and a password. Use a secure password and then click **create user**.

- Step 3: Add the user to the database by checking the **All Privileges** box and then click **next step**.

- Step 4: Write down the database name and user. Be sure to include the values of the hostname, username, databasename and the secure password you created. The host name will usually be called the localhost.

Lunarpages.com Custom cPanel:

If you are using Lunarpages.com, they have their own cPanel that requires a different process.

- Log into your Lunarpages account

- Go to the control panel

- On the left panel, you will find a button labeled "Go to LPCP", click on it.

- Go to MySQL Manager

- In the appropriate spaces, add a user name and database name, but don't make any adjustments to the host name as the default IP number. Just leave that as it is.

- On the database on the right, make a note of the IP address of the database. This is not the same as the default IP number in the previous step.

- Do not use "LOCALHOST" when you are modifying the WP-CONFIG.PHP. Use the DB IP number instead.

- Be certain you are using the full name of the database and user name when you are modifying the WP-CONFIG.PHP. This is usually "accountname_nameyoucreated".

- If you need more information, you can find it at http://wiki.lunarpages.com/Create_and_Delete_MySQL_Users_in_LPCP

phpMyAdmin:

If phpMyAdmin is installed on your server, use the following instructions to create a WordPress username and database. When you work on your computer, by using most Linux distributions you can install phpMyAdmin automatically.

(Instructions below are for phpMyAdmin 3.5. The user interface might vary a little bit in different versions, but this will give you a basic idea of what you will need to do.)

- In the dropdown menu on the left, look to see if a WordPress database already exists. If not, here is how you create one.

- Choose a name for your database. Most hosting services will require that the name begin with your username and an underscore. Be sure to check out the

28

requirements of your hosting company before you begin. This will prevent any modifications from needing to be done.

- In the **create database** field, enter the name that fits with the servers requirements. It is usually best to use the "utf8_" series, but you can use "utf8_unicode_ci" if you don't find that.

- Click the **create** button.

Creating the user:

- Click on the **phpMyAdmin** icon located at the top left. This will take you back to the main page.

- Click on the **users** tab and check to see if there is a user for WordPress.

- To add a new user, click **add user**.

- Choose a username. Something that identifies it as WordPress is a good idea. Enter the name in the **user name** field.

- Choose a strong password that is secure. Use numbers, symbols and a combination of upper and lower case letters for a strong password.

- Choose the **use text field** from the dropdown menu.

- Enter your secure password in the **password** field.

- In the **re-type password** field, re-enter the same password.

- Make a note of the user name and password you used to set this user up.

- Under **global privileges**, leave all of the options. The default options are exactly what you need here.

- Click **Go**.

These examples of manual uploads are meant to show you that a manual upload can be accomplished in a few simple steps, but many beginners may not feel entirely comfortable trying to do this. This is where easy installation with an easy to use cPanel will save you a lot of frustration, and the reason it is so heavily stressed in this book.

When you are a beginner, you want to keep things as simple as possible. Simple will allow you to get things done quickly, and with fewer technical difficulties. It is easy to make a mistake when you are an amateur, and difficult to find the mistake later when you need to fix it. Save yourself the headache and make sure you are getting a package with a hosting company that has auto install of WordPress.

Chapter Six:
Choose And Install A Theme

The theme is quite simply the appearance of your website; what developers would call the "front end". This is the part that the public sees, and the first impression you make on a visitor to your site. Themes will determine the layout of the content, the colors used and other design features. Different themes also have different functions, and you should read through the details of the themes you like before you decide on one. There are many themes that are offered for free, and you can customize the colors, fonts and other design elements used to make the theme fit you, and your businesses unique style.

First, you will need to log into your WordPress admin account. You can do this by going to wordpress.org or you can go to nameofyoursite.com/wp-admin. Initially, you will be taken to your homepage. You will likely see the default 2015 webpage. The defaults are very bland (and white), but that doesn't matter because you are going to choose a new theme that really shows what your business is about.

First, you need to log in to your dashboard. The dashboard is the control panel of your website, and the place where you will manage everything on your WordPress site. Here you can customize your site, add content and install plugins to add functionality.

To get to your dashboard, click on the name of your blog located at the top left of the screen. If you haven't named your site yet, the name will be your username. There are many options available to you for changing the theme on your WordPress site. Below are the most common and easiest ways to change the theme.

Adding A New Theme Using The WordPress Admin Panel:

- Find **appearance** on the menu located on the left

- Select **themes**

- Select **add new**

- You will be directed to a screen that will contain a variety of themes. If you have a theme in mind, you can use the search function to locate it. You can also use the filters to help you find a theme that will work best for your business.

- Click on the **preview** link to take the theme for a spin before you install it to your site. This will let you try out the features the theme offers and give you chance for you to decide if it is right for you.

- Once you have found the perfect them, click **install now** to apply it to your site.

- If you have a copy of a theme downloaded onto your computer, you can use that by clicking on the **upload** link located in the top row.

Adding A New Theme Using A cPanel:
(This option requires that you have a cPanel through your host, and that the files are compressed. Files that are compressed will end in .zip or .gz.)

- Download the zip file containing the theme to your computer.

- Log into your hosting account and go to your cPanel. Open your **themes** folder.

- Find your WordPress database. If it is installed in the root folder, it will be looking for "public_html/wp-content/themes". However, if it is installed in a subfolder, you will be looking for "public_html/wp-content/themes".

- Click **upload files**.

- In Step 1, select the .sip file that contains the theme.

- When the zip file has finished loading, click on it in the cPanel.

- On the panel located to the right, click **Extract File Contents**. This will expand the .zip file.

Adding The Theme Using FTP:

- Download theme archive

- Extract the files in the archive (follow instructions provided by the theme's author to preserve the structure of the directory)

- Use the FTP client to access your web server. Create a directory so you can save your themes in the wp-content/themes directory.

- Upload the theme files to the new directory.

Selecting Active Theme:

- Log into WordPress Admin Panels

- Go to **appearance**.

- Select **themes**.

- On the themes panel, roll your mouse over the thumbnails of the themes you are interested in to see the options available with the theme.

- Get more information by clicking **theme details**.

- Click **live preview** to take the theme for a test drive.

- If you like the theme, and want to apply it to your site, click on the **activate** button.

- The theme will immediately become active on your site.

You can drastically change the appearance of your site by simply changing the theme. You may periodically want to change the theme of your site simply because you will get bored with looking at the same site all the time. WordPress themes offer an easy and affordable way to give your site a facelift every few years. Themes are just one of the many reasons why WordPress makes managing a website so easy.

The beauty of WordPress is that it is open sourced, which means that you can rewrite the coding of the template to suit your needs or use a custom website. Both of these options will involve skills that the beginner will not have, but as your business grows, it is nice to have the option to be able to hire a professional web developer that can work within the foundation you have created to take your website to the next level.

Chapter Seven:
Set Up The Content And Make A Good First Impression

Now that you have your domain name set up, your web hosting ready, you have installed WordPress, and you have a designer look that was set up by using the perfect theme, it is time to add some content. Content is any text, picture, video or logo that you add to your site. Content is how search engines rank you and what encourages potential customers to explore your site.

The first thing to do here is to give your site a title and a tagline that match the message of your company mission statement.

- On the menu on the left, go to **customize**.

- Choose **Site Title and Tag Line**.

- Find the field for site title, and enter in your business name as the site title.

- Find the field for the tag line, and enter one sentence that best sums up your site and what it is about.

You can also adjust the header image. This can be an image that represents your company, like a logo.

Starting from your dashboard:

- Click **customize** on the menu to the left

- Choose **Header Image**

- Click **Add New Image**

- Upload the image you want on your header.

- Crop or drag the image to fit the header. Click on **crop image** or **skip cropping**.

- Click **Save and Publish**.

Now that you have the site title, tagline and header set, you are going to need to tell people about you. Your site will be made up of a series of pages, and you are going to need to set up a page as a static front page to act as your homepage.

To set up a homepage:

- Select pages from the menu on the left

- Click **Add New Page**

- Title it "Home" or "Homepage"

- Providing that the theme you are using allows you to customize the page, go to the **page attributes box** and select **template**.

- Add content to the page. This should include text that tells new visitors about your business. You can use the Add Media button to add photos and videos to the page, and stagger them with your text.

You are going to need to **set the page to be a static front page**.

- Go to the admin panel

- Select settings

- Select Reading

- Set the front page displays to be a static front page by:

  - Select the title of the page you designed to be your homepage in the drop down menu for the front page.

  - Save your changes

You can also use pages to tell people more about yourself or to add a contact form. You can set up pages within pages by selecting a parent page for subpages to live in.

For example, you may want to introduce the visitors to your site to your staff. However, you want to give each staff member their own page without creating a long list of pages that take up the front page and look ugly. To do this, you would set up a page for each staff member under a parent page.

- Go to pages

- Click **Add New Page**

- Title the page 'About Us'

- Use content that introduces people to the company, and invite them to browse through the staff profiles located in the About Us drop down menu

- Click **Publish**

What's that? You don't have a drop down menu on your page? You will.

- Go back to pages

- Click Add New Page

- Title the page with the staff member's name. You can also include their title or department if you want.

- I would recommend letting each staff member write up his or her profile, and I would use that as the text.

- Add a picture of the each member of your staff to their page using the **Add Media** button.

- In the Page Attributes box, choose About Us as the Parent dropdown menu.

- Click **Publish**.

Now, your About Us tab on the menu will act like a drop down menu, with each page you set up for the members of your staff showing up as a page in the menu.

Pages are a wonderful way to organize the information on your website. The best sites have content that is well arranged, makes sense to the viewer, doesn't overwhelm the viewer, and is easy to navigate and find information.

While pages are a fabulously easy way to build your site, they are limited in the functionality they provide. To really add some features that will impress visitors to your site, you will need to use plugins. You will find information about using those in the next chapter.

Chapter Eight:
The Power And The Beauty Of PlugIns

Wordpress.org offers you over 37,000 plugins that you can use to create the functionality you need for your site. This is where you will find options for adding an online store, optimizing your SEO goals, and building pages that store content aimed at engaging your customers.

Plugins are not available on Wordpress.com sites. You must have a Wordpress.org, which you will only have if you set up hosting outside of WordPress.

Your site will have two plugins automatically included. These are:

Akismet: This plugin is designed to manage spam comments. If the comment looks like it could be spam, Akismet will catch it and drop it into a folder that prevents the comment from being posted publicly. However, it will automatically clean the old stuff out by deleting it after it has been sitting there for 15 days.

Hello Dolly: There seems to be a great debate over the usefulness of this plugin. Most people just delete it to get rid of the "Hello Dolly" that always seems to be in the way. It seems that this plugin, which was WordPress' first plugin, may have been designed to help people publish their first post. However, WordPress is so easy to use that most people feel that they really don't need it.

To Delete Hello Dolly:

- On the left menu, under settings, click on plugins

- Check the box next to Hello Dolly, and then click Deactivate.

- Again check the box next to Hello Dolly, and then click Delete.

That's it! Good-bye Dolly. Remember that you must deactivate the plugin before you can delete it.

To browse the thousands of plugins available to you on WordPress, you can visit the official WordPress Plugins Directory (www.wordpress.org/plugins/). Look at the plugins that you think can help your business run smoother, and offer your customers the most benefit. Remember, you want to add value to the site. This is also where you will find e-commerce applications to run an online store from your website.

To add some plugins that you might find to be more useful:

- Sign into your WordPress admin panel

- On the menu to the left, under settings, click on plugins

- Click **Add New**

- Find the plugin that you want to add to your site

  o Click on **details** and print out the instructions

  o Click **Install Now** to complete the installation

- A pop up window will ask you to confirm that you wish to install the plugin.

- If this is your first time installing a plugin, you will need to enter your FTP login credentials for your server. If you don't know this information, you will be able to get it from your web-hosting company.

- Click **Install**

- Check the installation screen after the install has completed to see if it was successful or if there were any problems.

- If the install was a success, click **Activate Plugin**

Sometimes, it makes more sense to do install the plugin manually. In instances where you:

- Want to control the placement of the plugin

- Server doesn't allow automatic installation

- The plugin isn't included in the official WordPress directory

In these instances, you are better off having someone who knows what they are doing help you. These processes require a basic knowledge of FTP, and can put your site at risk if you install a plugin that isn't compatible or originates from a source that is unreliable.

Plugins are a fantastic way to add functionality to your site, and the variety of functions they provide will give you endless opportunities to customize your site and build something truly special.

Conclusion

Thank you again for downloading this book!

I hope this book was able to help you to design and publish a beautiful website that will take your business to the next level, and that you enjoyed learning a little bit about how websites are created. It is also my sincerest hope that you are able to take a great deal of pride in the fact that you created your own website. It wasn't so long ago that the ability to build a website required at least some technical knowledge that many of us didn't have the opportunity to acquire. However, you just built your own website, and regardless of how much easier technology has made this it is still a major accomplishment.

The next step is to work on getting the word out about your shiny new website. You can use social media or include it on business cards. Put that website's URL out there every chance you get. You should also continue to explore the wonders of WordPress. Who knows what you will be able to accomplish once you acquire some intermediate knowledge? The website you just built can be an achievement of your final goal or it could be only the beginning. Should you choose to continue learning about WordPress, you may learn some coding and one day you could be contributing plugins on the open source network that WordPress is built on. Imagine that! Today a little webpage, tomorrow the world!

Finally, if you enjoyed this book, please take the time to share your thoughts and post a review on Amazon. It'd be greatly appreciated!

Thank you and good luck!

www.ingramcontent.com/pod-product-compliance
Lightning Source LLC
Chambersburg PA
CBHW070904070326
40690CB00009B/1986